DESERT SPRINGS PUBLISHING
CUSTOM BOOKS
78-365 Highway 111, Suite 340, La Quinta, California 92253
Telephone 760-219-7008 • www.desertspringspublishing.com

Printed in China / First Edition Printing, 2008

Library of Congress Control Number Data on File with Publisher.

ISBN# 972757295
ISBN# 9780972757294

Wally Wheeler — 80-345 Larkhall Court, Indio, CA 92201
Telephone 1-877-966-3359 • www.howtothrowagolfclub.com

Design Network — 11860 Pomelo Drive, Desert Hot Springs, CA 92240
Telephone 760-774-7011 • E-mail: roger@designnetwork.us

Written by Wally Wheeler
Illustrations and Book Design by Roger A. Dean
Marketing Consultant, Gayl Biondi
Publisher, Victoria Bailey

Acknowledgement

The idea for this book originated in my brain about twenty years ago, just how I can't remember. While playing golf with Gus Patzner, an excellent musician who could play about any instrument made and, incidentally, could make music from a 2x4, he exclaimed, "I've got those golf club throwing blues!"

That got my mind going. One night several weeks later just before bedtime, I had an inspiration to write the words to a song titled "I've Got Those Golf Club Throwing Blues," which took me about 5 minutes to write and compose. Gus wrote the music for it and I had a big band arrangement made.

Sometime later, the idea for a story flowed through my mind and that's when "how to throw a *!!?★*@!!?★!&*★#!! golf club" was born.

Commercial artist Roger K. Dean was asked to illustrate cartoons for the book and it sat on the shelf for years as I was busy with my medical practice and other endeavors. Retirement came on May 31, 2006. I dusted off the manuscript and started up once again. Roger had retired, so I contracted his son, Roger A. Dean, to contribute with the illustrations. He has contributed more cartoons, gathered them together, and we have published what you are reading today. These two artists are tops in their field. Isaac Aceves also contributed some ideas and concepts regarding the cartoon sketches. Thanks to Chuck Pryor (aka Terrible Charles) for scripting the excellent foreword. We have all had fun and enjoyment putting this project together. We hope you enjoy it as well.

Finally, many thanks to my wife Muriel Wheeler who spent many hours typing up and correcting the manuscript.

Wally Wheeler

Wally Wheeler

Wally Wheeler
The Even Tempered Gentleman

FOREWORD

Golf is a game that can be played all your life for social and business reasons and with persons of greatly varying abilities. Yet, maybe its most profound benefit is that it provides opportunities for unrestrained, impromptu and passionate expressions both verbal and physical.

We know that golf can be a "model for life" as it teaches and demands personal integrity, honesty, perseverance, character, ethics and, hopefully growth and maturity. Frequently, a golfer's patience and maturity are stretched far beyond the acceptable limits of normal behavior. Psychiatrists love golfers with their split personalities, insatiable expectancies and absurd rationalizations.

It requires a "spiritual discipline" to achieve an acceptable balance in golf, but normally we suffer "divine discontent" as we always dream of what could be and are never satisfied. Golf, like life, is no place for the naive and reluctant personalities.

For these reasons and many other justifications, the ultimate expression in golf (throwing clubs) should be studied and then verbalized in writing. Who better to do that than Dr. Wheeler, an even tempered gentleman, always in control of his emotions with a view of life that is real and concerned? Yet, on the golf course he was a fierce competitor, hated to not perform better than his ability and would occasionally say, "Oh, darn it!"

My introduction to golf was in 1937. I was nine years old, and my first club throwing incident was about 1948 while in college at the University of Southern California. My baseball playing buddies were a bad influence on me. Of course, my idol as a club thrower was the great Tommy Bolt. Casting his driver into the lake on the eighteenth hole at the U.S. Open at Cherry Hills in 1960 was the ultimate in golfing expressions.

Fortunately, I have become a club throwing legend at clubs to which I have belonged and among my closest companions. They will remember me long after they have forgotten who the club champion was, although my motive for club throwing was not recognition, but excellence in anything does create respect.

Young golfers should not be encouraged or allowed to throw clubs. You have to earn that right after years of servitude to the game and the uncompromising punishment of the "Great God of Golf." The older and infirmed club throwing golfer should always have a person in the foursome who can retrieve clubs.

Club throwing is an art and many times I have I been asked to award style points when others have "let it fly." The most important criteria is that club throwing must be honest, sincere and with one hundred percent effort.

Dr. Wheeler has provided a remarkable service with his book on club throwing and it should be required reading for anyone who takes the game seriously. Perhaps he will consider a sequel called "The Obscenities That Accompany Club Throwing." Good luck and good reading.

Chuck Pryor (aka Terrible Charles)

PREFACE

This manual describing the art of throwing a golf club has been waiting to be published since the first Scotsman, in frustration, flung his club into the heather on the Old Course in St. Andrews, Scotland.

This book is not a "Stuffed Turkey," but is short and concise. No extra words to make it longer. No fat, skin or stuffing. Just good white and dark meat.

It is my aim to get all club throwers to band together as one to improve their skills, to better themselves, and to raise the art of club throwing to a higher level. Have we all been in the closet? Perhaps. This dissertation will explain why, where, how, and whether to bring all club throwers to their rightful place in the annals of golf. Amen! Oh, I love composing this book. I can finally get even with that ✳!!?★✳@!\?★!&✳★✦#!\ golf club.

We're on our way! In this book I also share my time tested secrets and the inner mechanics of correctly throwing a golf club.

You don't have to be crazy to play golf, but it helps. It's amazing that anyone in his right mind plays golf. It must tell something about basic human intelligence when a game that is so frustrating is played by so many people. We must be idiots!

Families, sisters, brothers, neighbors and nations can't get along with each other but 14 million golfers can unite with only one thought in mind...I'm going to beat that game or else!

You've heard the golfer who says, " I just play for the fun of it." My eye! We all play to win!

Oh, you say you don't? Come on now. Don't you smile inwardly just a tiny bit when the other guy three putts for a 6 and you get a 5? Haven't you ever felt a smattering of joy when his ball lands in the lake or out of bounds? Of course you have.

No one will ever be able to adequately describe the lure of this game that can be so frustrating, yet at times so rewarding an endeavor. "Game"? No way!

How many times, with knees shaking, palms sweating, knuckles white and heart pounding, have I marched to the first tee with a crowd of vultures looking on, and prayed, "Dear God, just this once let me get off the first tee alive!"

Seems like God was out playing golf Himself because I'm sure He wouldn't have let me dribble yards off the front of the tee into the only lake on the whole golf course!

You, too? Welcome, Brother-Sister.

We must unite and learn how to throw the *!!?★*@!!?★!&*★#!! golf clubs correctly!

Yours is the decision to throw the club. You should do it properly. There is a wrong way and a right way. You will learn the right way. When the urge comes, and surely it will, you will at last have proper club throwing fundamentals.

Club throwing can be a worthy endeavor. Properly done, it gives you class, a certain esteem. Believe me, you will be admired, imitated, and immortalized. Learn to do it well. Be the best in your flight...your club...and yes, perhaps, the best in the world!

You don't have to be a participant to enjoy the art of throwing golf clubs. It also makes a great spectator sport. Stand back and observe your golf buddies. Watch the frustration — the redness of face, the building of tension — until finally the golfer lets go and launches the golf club into space.

My qualifications to expound on the art of club throwing are as follows.

Some sixty years or so ago, at age seven, my dad introduced me to the game of golf. We started at the local driving range and as I grew older and larger, I caddied for him and his friends.

Later I started to play on gravel patches called golf courses. Many times during the summers when I worked at Dad's dye factory, he and I would leave soon after lunch to call on customers. After one call, off to the golf course we would go. It was easy to finish 18 holes and get back to the factory to close at five.

My dad loved golf. Unfortunately, I don't remember much about his game, but I do recall that never was a curse word heard, and never was a club seen flying from his hands.

The same can't be said of some of his friends, or of me. I can't remember exactly when I threw my first club, but many clubs have since left my hands for a ride through the air, but never when anyone was around.

Well, maybe once when my wife was with me, but I never had the guts when playing with anyone else.

You needn't be that chicken!

Come on, now. It's time for all golf club throwers to show their true colors. Stand up for your rights — throw those *!!?★*@!!?★!&*★#!! clubs with pride! Let those clubs know you mean business.

Maybe next time that club will hit the ball where you want it, not where it wants it.

THROWING A CLUB WITH PRIDE

Don't let another ✳‼?★✳@‼?★¡&✳⬧#‼ club get by you without the punishment it deserves just because others may be watching. Many clubs deserve to be thrown. Any club that shanks seven balls in a row — yes, seven — deserves to be thrown. Three of those balls went out-of-bounds and were never heard from again.
Serves them right!

The first ✳‼?★✳@‼?★¡&✳⬧#‼ golf club that ever left my hands was probably at the tender age of 11 or 12 years old. Many clubs during the following 43 years sailed into the stratosphere.

Recently, while making an approach shot to the 18th green on what could have been quite a successful round (if you consider a 78 successful, and I do), disaster struck. I got down in three. Blasting away at the green with my 8 iron, it shanked and went out of bounds. Another ball, shank No.2. Another ball, shank No.3, etc., etc., etc., etc., through seven balls.

Who would give up? I couldn't. The eightball landed on the green, and two putts later a 19 was carded, giving me a 92 for the round. My boiling point was rapidly approaching, but temptation was resisted.
That ✳‼?★✳@‼?★¡&✳⬧#‼ 8 iron never left my hands, but it should have. It deserved annihilation! Shank after shank!
What was wrong?

Golf Tip: *After years of reading golf books, studying and experimenting, I have finally found out what causes my shanking. (Pay attention. This tip will not be found in other golf books.) You must keep your weight on the heels. If you lean forward, the hosel hits the ball, causing a shank. Of course, there may be other causes for shanking, but this seems to be the Number One cause.*

I've observed club throwing throughout the years, and the majority of throwers have no class, no professionalism. My greatest throw happened one hot summer day while practicing alone.

I remember it as if it was yesterday! Three shots in a row were hit out of bounds to the left, and the next two into the water on the right. I grabbed the grip of that driver with both hands and turned clockwise 185 degrees, then counter-clockwise with ever increasing speed. Stepping forward one step, with a grunt, a mighty heave and an incantation appropriate to the moment, I released that *!!?★*@!!?★!&★★#!! instrument of torture.

It flew from my hands and soared away, whistling and vibrating. Finally it landed and kept skidding on the ground.

Any remorse?

No!

Absolutely none!

It was too great a feeling. That's the best thing about club throwing.

Sitting here reliving those exciting moments makes me feel wonderful!

Frankly and modestly, my throwing form is good. It has class, but it can't compare with Terrible Charles. He is a super star, a one-in-a-lifetime throwing artist. Terrible Charles has it all. He's a man's man (also a lady's) — handsome and debonair with an Adonis build and 100% Park Avenue attitude.

Terrible Charles' throwing form remains unsurpassed. Instinctively he knew when, where, and how to throw his club. On one momentous occasion, during a club tournament, he teed up on the first tee, wound up and let go with a might swing. It would have been a tremendous shot had it gone straight. It would have landed on the green 325 yards away. But, no, that wasn't the fate of that particular ball. It started out straight, hooked left over a row of oleanders, sailed across the road, and was never seen again.

With the proper selection of words, Terrible Charles banged the club head on the tee marker, breaking said club head. But that was not all! What? There is more? Yes!

Synchronizing his movement, he made a forward lunge, hurling that club into orbit 160 feet down the fairway. The whole gallery at the first tee was awestruck. It was the most magnificent display of sheer power, coordination, rage, verbal expression and finesse ever witnessed. Yes! And never to be performed again. Terrible Charles threw other clubs but he never exceeded the form displayed on this occasion. What a guy to admire and emulate!

As a reward, I awarded Terrible Charles the first "Order of the Broken Club, Triple Bogie," the highest award in club throwing. My efforts to duplicate his feat failed miserably. I just didn't have it.

Terrible Charles was a great fellow, and a great golfer. He'd won the club championship several times. I dare say the time I have spent studying the art of club throwing exceeds that of anyone else. I have observed club throwing, have thrown clubs myself, and have spent hours obtaining and analyzing data on the art. Interestingly, I have never seen an amateur woman throw a golf club although I have played golf with many of the fair set. Why? Who knows? They do get mad. Perhaps it's time for all you women golfers to let go.

Now, down to the nitty-gritty. As with anything scientific, the complex art of golf club throwing can be analyzed.

The fundamental parts are:

Equipment
Mental attitude
Grip
Stance
Windup
Release
Launching angle
Follow through
Speed
Verbal expression
Retrieval
Finale

EQUIPMENT

As with anything, the better the equipment the better the results. A $10.00 chain store putter just isn't going to do the job as well as a $125.00 jewel. The more expensive $135.00 seven iron imparts a warm inner glow as it flies through the air. Is it going to break? Disappear forever?

Swing, weight, total weight, stiffness or shaft and length all have an effect. This is of importance only to the professional club thrower. To the average golfer it has little influence.

Throw whatever you're holding in your hand. At such a critical moment who cares about club selection?

MENTAL ATTITUDE

One must be mentally alert with all brain systems "Go." When the aggravation occurs, your reaction must be immediate. You will never be a good club thrower if you go about the golf course looking at the flowers and the opposite sex.

You don't have to have the killer instinct, but it helps. Your mind must be ever ready for action. As the game of golf changes all too quickly, you must be mentally ready at a moment's notice.

An "It's only a game!" attitude will get you nowhere, but the one that will help you attain your highest club throwing ambitions is, "You can't do that to me, you *‼?★*@‼?★!&*★#‼ golf club!"

GRIP

One-Handed Grip

Get a grip! This is most important. A loose grip is worthless, as is hands apart. There is the one-hand grip, but, personally, I like the two-hand VARDON grip. It gives me better control on special occasions. Each style has its aficionados. A baseball type of grip, however, is basically sound, and will serve you quite well.

STANCE

A must. Both feet on the ground. You will only get into trouble with both feet in the air. A closed or open stance makes no difference. Get a firm footing. Having cleats on your shoes will add a good extra ten feet. You'll look pretty silly if you slip and land on your butt. Besides, you will get no distance at all.

23

WINDUP

The windup is the most variable of all elements in the throwing of a ✳!!?★✳@!!?★!&✳✦#!! golf club.

The standard for a right-handed player is to plant your feet firmly in the turf (see Stance), turn your torso clockwise as far as possible, wind up your body as tight as a spring, then immediately unwind rapidly.

It is absolutely essential to have both feet firmly planted so as to build up energy in the tightness of your turn. This contracts the large muscles in your legs and back so when you unwind, your body is rotating at maximum speed.

RELEASE / DIRECTION

Timing in the release of the club cannot be emphasized enough. This you must work on to gain perfection. It may take hours. You will lose untold distance if you release either too early or too late. The instant of release is critical. A poorly timed release may cause your club to fly at or even hit your golf buddies, and they won't be amused.

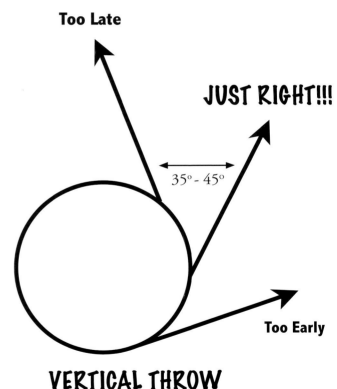

Too Late

JUST RIGHT!!!

35° - 45°

Too Early

VERTICAL THROW

STANCE

Release is easier with one hand. The extra distance you get with a two-hand grip, however, makes additional hours of practice rewarding. It is worth it!

The admiration of others at your skill is only one of the benefits of practice. Others include style, body form, and above all else, an increase of distance.

Release timing has a direct bearing on **DIRECTION**, an element of club throwing you must never forget. One incident worth mentioning comes to mind. During a round in a foursome with which I was engaged in combat, one golfer was having an off day. Nothing went right. At the seventh green, he missed a short putt. He turned crimson with rage and let fly his putter. His form, language, facial expression, grip and release, were perfect—nothing to criticize. He failed, however, to consider direction, and for this mistake, there was a price to pay.

The club landed high up in an extremely dense tree with leaves like thorned Christmas holly. The putter slithered into the thickness like a snake after a gopher.

None of us could see where it was located and no one dared climb that massive tree. When leaving the green, the hapless golfer was heard muttering something about the ancestry of both the putter and the tree.

REMEMBER DIRECTION! You must consider direction, the most important part of all golf club throwing fundamentals. If a lake is nearby, that is a first rate option. A thickly branched tree is almost as good. Don't do as I saw one lady pro do. She tossed the incorrigible club upward. This is not good, for it can hit you on the way down. Be absolutely positive no one is in the line of flight. If you hit someone, expect a nasty visit from his very unfriendly lawyer. If you throw uphill, your distance is sacrificed. My preference is downhill, especially if there is a lake at the bottom. It adds to your distance, and the splash stimulates your auditory and visual senses.

LAUNCHING ANGLE

The angle of launch is the angle between the horizontal plane and the arm when the club is released. I get my greatest distance at about 30 degrees. Each person must experiment to determine his proper angle. The greater the angle, the greater the distance, up to about 45 degrees, at which point the club goes higher in the air away from the frustrated golfer. A negative angle or an angle below the horizon promptly puts the club on the ground—really not a bad place! Considering the amount of energy stored up in the club at the instant of release, there is naturally a preferred angle of launch for the maximum distance.

At a moment like this, who cares?

Wind up and let 'er go. With practice, subconsciously you'll know what to do.

FOLLOW THROUGH

In hitting a golf ball, the follow through motion after impact is almost as important as the back swing. It's the same in throwing a golf club. If you stop your turn at the moment you release the club, you will lose 20-30 percent of your distance. Continue your arch, letting your hands follow the club as long as you can, before turning. This is very important.

SPEED FORMULA

In the formula:

ke = kinetic energy
v = velocity
m = mass or weight
ke = $\frac{1}{2}$ mv^2

It is easily seen for those mathematically oriented that speed is the important item here.

For example:

let m = 2

let

v = 2
ke = $\frac{1}{2}$ x 2 x 2 x 2 = 4

If the mass is doubled to 4, then:

ke = $\frac{1}{2}$ x 4 x 2 x 2 = 8

If, in the above example, mass or weight remain at two, and velocity is doubled to 4, great things happen:

ke = $\frac{1}{2}$ x 2 x 4 x 4 = 16 !

ke is now **4** times the original value of **4!**

LESSON: Forget the weight. We want speed!!! Get that club going as fast as you can. The results will astound you!

VERBAL EXPRESSION

What you say at the time of release has more effect on the distance you achieve than one might imagine.
It must be said with **VIGOR!** You have to be mad to get the best results.

    If it's distance you're after, the faster and louder you express yourself the better.

    My preference is *!!?★*@!!?★!&*★#!! Of course, you may prefer not to chieve any distance to speak of at all.
If this is the case, just toss, gently drop or flip the golf club aside, saying...

" Oh - - - - !!! "

RETRIEVAL

Retrieval can be very embarrassing, especially if your club lands in the lake or on another golfer's head.

If you've dumped the club, lean over nonchalantly, and pick it up as if you were doing it a favor.

If you have pitched it some distance away, there are six things you can do:

1. With head high and chin up, stride over and get it.

2. Slink over and surreptitiously pick it up.

3. If thrown into the lake or into a bush, sneak back and get it after dark.

4. If you have a caddie, bribe him.

5. If you are fortunate enough to have a golf cart, drive around aimlessly for awhile before going over to retrieve the club inconspicuously.

6. Or just forget it! That's a very hard thing to do if the club cost two hundred bucks or more.

Maybe, just maybe, someone in the foursome behind you may turn it in at the pro shop.

Personally, my favorite is Number 1.

No *!!?★*@!!?★!&★★#!! golf club is going to make a jackass out of me!

35

I have included a chart below to guide and assist you with your decision
WHEN TO or, WHEN NOT TO throw a ✱!!?★✱@!?★!&✱✦#!! golf club.

PLAYING PARTNER	YOUR REACTION	THROW
1. Girlfriend	Foolish Grin	NO!
2. Fiancée	Occasional Damn	No
3. Wife (of one year)	Frequent Damn	Almost Rarely
4. Wife (of 25 years)	✱!!?★✱@!?★!&✱✦#!!	YES!
5. Son or Daughter (10-12 years)	Occasional Grunt	No
6. Daughter (age 18)	Occasional Grunt	No
7. Daughter-in-law	Occasional Grunt	No
8. Son (age 18)	✱!!?★✱@!?★!&✱✦#!!	No
9. Son-in-law	✱!!?★✱@!?★!&✱✦#!!	YES!
10. Clergy	None	NO!
11. Banker	None	No
12. Client	None, unless client starts	Maybe?
13. Golfing Buddies	Anything Goes!	Always!
14. Boss	None	No
15. Employee	✱!!?★✱@!?★!&✱✦#!!	YES!
16. Mixed Foursome	Occasional Grunt (Perhaps an "Oh, Hell")	No
17. Club Pro	Mimic	Maybe
18. President of the USA	Weak Smile	NO!

Regrets? **Heck no!**

The club deserves to be thrown. After all, it wasn't your fault the ball shanked into the lake, hit out of bounds, topped, sliced, hooked, etc., etc.

Hold your head high. Harbor no regrets. Keep a stiff upper lip. If you have thrown the club with class and distinction, other golfers will talk about you, emulate you, and even envy you. You'll be a hero — if not publicly, certainly privately. Remember Terrible Charles. The whole membership of the men's golf club envied him. And justly so. What a guy! What class! What a club thrower!

COMPETITIVE CLUB THROWING

At the time of this book's writing there are no organized competitive club throwing events. I anticipate that this will change due to the heightened awareness of the merits of club throwing. I therefore propose the following items be considered when scoring competitive club throwing. Each element is valued individually, receiving a rating of 1-5 points, and a perfect score is 50 points. The elements consist of:

1. Stance
2. Grip
3. Windup
4. Unwinding
5. Release

6. Follow-through
7. Facial contortions
8. Verbal expression
9. Artistic appearance
10. Distance

Actually, in an honest-to-goodness club throwing contest, distance is the only practical consideration, because it can be measured objectively. If you try to include all the other items, beware! You may lose friends.

In a national event, each item must be evaluated for the fine points listed above. Golf club throwing is an art and a beautiful creative expression when done correctly. Complete attention must be paid to each detail.

However, in our society, the score is too often the main consideration when distance is the thing.

FINALE

To end this dissertation, the following story is apropos. A certain golfer (to remain unnamed) had a particularly frustrating day. Everything that could go wrong went wrong. He took it as long as he could, but finally cracked after hitting his last remaining ball into the water in front of the 18th green. Grabbing his bag of clubs with a masterful heave, he arched bag and clubs into the lake, and stomped off cursing with a curious smile on his face.

A few minutes later, he marched back to the lake with a scowl on his face, cursing even worse than before. Wading into the lake, he finally found his golf bag and clubs and, after extracting his car keys and wallet, threw the bag violently back into the water and stalked off into oblivion.

With this insight and knowledge concerning how to throw a golf club, I am anxious to hear your personal stories. Send them to me as they may make up a second edition on golf club throwing. There lurks in the back of my mind a golf club throwing contest. We could have regional qualifying rounds leading to meets. Perhaps a sponsor will surface. Once a year I propose a US Open Golf Club Throwing contest.

I can see this build into something big with regular tours, international meets, best-throwers-of-the-region with top money winners, and even our own GCTA (Golf Club Throwing Association).

Tell me the kind of distance you get, your favorite throwing club, and anything of interest to fellow club throwers.

Send your stories, suggestions, and experiences to:

Wally Wheeler
80345 Larkhall Court
Indio, California 92201
bandwheel@aol.com
1-877-966-3359

EPILOGUE

This guide to throwing a *‼?★*@‼?★!&*★#‼ golf club is only a beginning — a foot in the door, so to speak — of a new frontier. There will be other pioneers to build upon my dream. Years from now sports historians will look back and record, "There once was a man who had his own Camelot. He dared to tread on virgin ground where others dared not." A shining moment, a true Camelot! A book written on:

how to throw a
‼?★@‼?★!&*★#‼
golf club!!!

Actually, I have an even better recommendation than throwing clubs...

Don't get mad, get even.

Break the *‼?★*@‼?★!&*★#‼ thing !!!!

But only if you can afford it!

OUCH!!!

how to throw a
!!?★@'!?★!&*★#'!
golf club!!!

This book has been written for entertainment only.

There is no intent to indicate throwing a golf club is proper or advisable.

Comments are not necessarily based on facts.